ADAPTED TO SUR

ANIMALS THAT RUN

Angela Royston

Raintree

Chicago, Illinois

Edited by Dan Nunn, Rebecca Rissman, and Helen Cox Cannons
Designed by Jo Hinton-Malivoire
Original illustrations © Capstone Global Library Ltd
Picture research by Mica Brancic
Production by Helen McCreath
Originated by Capstone Global Library Ltd
Printed and bound in China

17 16 15 14 13
10 9 8 7 6 5 4 3 2 1

Library of Congress Cataloging-in-Publication Data
Royston, Angela, 1945- author.
   Animals that run / Angela Royston.
      pages cm.—(Adapted to survive)
   Includes bibliographical references and index.
   ISBN 978-1-4109-6150-1 (hb)—ISBN 978-1-4109-6157-0 (pb) 1. Animal locomotion—Juvenile literature. 2. Animals—Adaptation—Juvenile literature. I. Title.
QL751.5.R695 2014
591.47'9—dc23   2013017640

Acknowledgments
The author and publisher are grateful to the following for permission to reproduce copyright material: Corbis pp. 25, 29 bottom right (© George H.H. Huey); Getty Images p. 27 (Universal Images Group/Auscape); Naturepl.com pp. 6 (© Jabruson), 7 (© Bryan and Cherry Alexander), 8, 20 (© Tony Heald), 13 (© B&S Draker), 14 (© Eric Baccega), 16 (© Carol Walker), 22 (© Visuals Unlimited), 24 (© Bernard Castelein), 26 (© Ingo Arndt); Shutterstock pp. 5, 29 top right (© Villiers Steyn), 15 (© Dennis Donohue), 19 (© Howard Sandler), 23 (© Linda Bucklin), 29 bottom left (© Eric Isselee); SuperStock pp. 4 (Belinda Images), 9 (Gallo Images), 10 (Corbis), 11, 12 (Minden Pictures), 17 (imagebroker.net/Alessandra Sarti/imag), 18 (age fotostock/Berndt Fischer), 21, 29 top left (age fotostock).

Cover photograph of a horse running reproduced with permission of Getty Images (Iconica/Arctic-Images).

We would like to thank Michael Bright for his invaluable help in the preparation of this book.

Some words are shown in bold, **like this.** You can find out what they mean by looking in the glossary.

CONTENTS

GOOD AT RUNNING

Some large animals, such as horses and camels, can run very fast. Some small animals can also run fast for their size. Why and how do they run so well?

RUNNING TO SURVIVE

Animals run fast because it helps them **survive**. Many animals **stalk** and chase other animals to eat. They need to run fast to catch their **prey**. Most of the animals they chase can also run fast, but not all.

gnu

wild dogs

Hunters pick on young and injured animals that cannot run so well, like this newborn baby reindeer.

ADAPTED TO RUN

Adaptations are special things about an animal's body that help it **survive**. Fast runners often have a slender, **streamlined** body and long legs. Running takes a lot of energy.

impala

Champion Runners

Cheetahs can reach speeds of 70 miles (113 kilometers) per hour. That is as fast as a car on the highway!

CHEETAHS

The cheetah is the fastest land animal on Earth. It runs fast to catch its **prey**. Its spine stretches and bends so that its strong back legs cover the ground in huge strides. Its long tail helps it balance.

long tail

Faster than a Sports Car

A cheetah can reach its top speed in just 3 seconds! After sprinting less than a minute, however, it runs out of breath and collapses.

GAZELLES AND PRONGHORNS

Gazelles are small antelope. They can run fast and change direction quickly. This helps them escape from cheetahs and other **predators**. Pronghorns can sprint at up to 62 miles (100 kilometers) per hour, but they can also keep running for several miles at 40 miles (65 kilometers) per hour.

gazelle

pronghorn

WOLVES

Wolves often run long distances, hunting for food. Wolves have long legs and big front feet. They spread their toes and use their claws to grip the ground. Wolves often hunt together to run down **prey**.

A group of wolves is called a pack.

Long Distance Champion

Wolves can run up to 60 miles (96 kilometers) in one night. That is farther than two marathon races!

GALLOPING HORSES

In the past, wild horses ran fast to escape from wolves and other **predators**. They have long, thin legs, and strong **muscles** in their shoulders and hips. Today, the fastest horses are racehorses.

Racehorses are trained to run fast. They can gallop at up to 43 miles (70 kilometers) per hour!

HARES

long back legs

Hares are well **adapted** for moving fast. Their power comes from their longer back legs and back feet. They quickly hop to escape from danger. A snowshoe hare has extra-long back feet. These act like **snowshoes** to stop the hare from sinking into the snow.

Snowshoe hares live in parts of North America that are snowy all winter.

OSTRICHES

Most birds escape from **predators** by flying away, but ostriches are too big and heavy to fly. Instead, they use their long, thin legs to run away from lions and other predators.

Ostriches use their wings to help them slow down.

DID YOU KNOW?
An ostrich can run at up to 43 miles (70 kilometers) per hour. That is faster than any other two-legged animal, including humans!

FASTEST LIZARD

Lizards run to escape from **predators**. A collared lizard is a very fast lizard. Instead of running on all four legs, it stands up and runs on its two back legs. It uses its long tail to help it balance when it runs.

A collared lizard takes huge strides on its back legs. Its long claws grip the ground.

Fast Dinosaur?

A collared lizard looks like a dinosaur called Compsognathus. Many scientists think that Compsognathus was the fastest of all the dinosaurs.

CRABS

A crab moves fast to escape from danger. It has eight legs, four on each side of its body. It usually runs sideways, because that is how its legs bend. Ghost crabs are one of the fastest moving crabs. When they move fast, they lift their four back legs off the ground and run on their four front legs.

Fastest Crab
A ghost crab can run at almost 13 feet (4 meters) per second. That's fast!

INSECTS

Most insects fly away from danger, but wingless insects cannot. Some run fast instead. An Australian tiger beetle runs 171 times its own length in a second. If people could do the same, we would sprint at an amazing 746 miles (1,200 kilometers) per hour!

A tiger beetle moves fast by running on just two of its six legs.

Australian tiger beetle

ANIMAL CHALLENGE

1. Most crabs do not run fast. What do they have instead that protects them from **predators** such as fish?

2. Which do you think can run faster—an elephant or a giraffe? Why?

3. Many animals that live on flat, grassy plains can run fast. Why do you think that is?

Invent your own fast animal. You can use the **adaptations** shown in the photos, or you can make up some of your own.

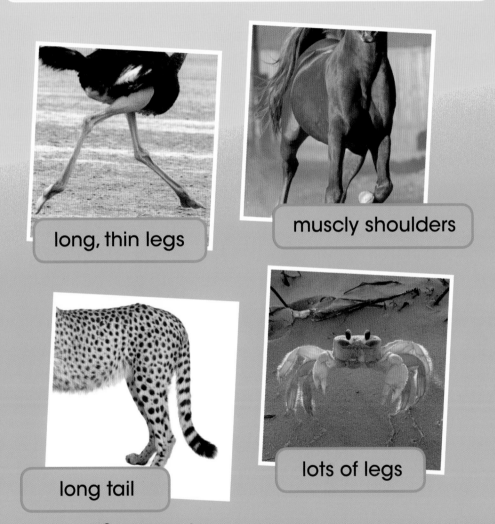

long, thin legs

muscly shoulders

long tail

lots of legs

Answers to Animal Challenge

1. Crabs have a hard shell and two sharp claws to protect themselves from predators.
2. Giraffes have long, slim legs and can run faster than elephants. Elephants are heavy, with stout legs.
3. There are few trees and bushes on grassy plains, so there are few places to hide. Animals have to run away from danger.

GLOSSARY

adaptation special thing about an animal's body that helps it survive in a particular way or in a particular habitat

adapted well suited to a particular activity or way of living

muscle fleshy part of the body that makes a particular part of the body move

predator animal that hunts and kills other animals for food

prey animal that is hunted and eaten by another animal

snowshoes large flat shoes that help a person walk over snow without sinking into it

stalk follow an animal or person, often without being seen

streamlined smooth, pointed shape that moves through air or water easily

survive manage to go on living

FIND OUT MORE

BOOKS

Gagne, Tammy. *Cheetahs.* Mankato, Minn.: Capstone, 2012.

Meinking, Mary. *Predator Vs. Prey* (series). Chicago: Raintree, 2011.

Murray, Julie. *Fastest Animals.* Edina, Minn.: ABDO, 2010.

Rake, Jody Sullivan. *Speed, Strength, and Stealth* (Animal Weapons and Defenses). Mankato, Minn: Capstone, 2012.

WEB SITES

FactHound offers a safe, fun way to find Internet sites related to this book. All of the sites on FactHound have been researched by our staff.

Here's all you do:
Visit www.facthound.com
Type in this code: 9781410961501

INDEX